S. 1110, THE ENGINE COOLANT AND ANTIFREEZE BITTERING AGENT ACT OF 2005

United States Congress Senate
Committee on Commerce, Science, and Transportation, Subcommittee on Consumer Affairs, Product Safety, and Insurance

The BiblioGov Project is an effort to expand awareness of the public documents and records of the U.S. Government via print publications. In broadening the public understanding of government and its work, an enlightened democracy can grow and prosper. Ranging from historic Congressional Bills to the most recent Budget of the United States Government, the BiblioGov Project spans a wealth of government information. These works are now made available through an environmentally friendly, print-on-demand basis, using only what is necessary to meet the required demands of an interested public. We invite you to learn of the records of the U.S. Government, heightening the knowledge and debate that can lead from such publications.

Included are the following Collections:

Budget of The United States Government
Presidential Documents
United States Code
Education Reports from ERIC
GAO Reports
History of Bills
House Rules and Manual
Public and Private Laws
Code of Federal Regulations
Congressional Documents
Economic Indicators
Federal Register
Government Manuals
House Journal
Privacy act Issuances
Statutes at Large

S. Hrg. 109–377

S. 1110, THE ENGINE COOLANT AND ANTIFREEZE BITTERING AGENT ACT OF 2005

HEARING

BEFORE THE

SUBCOMMITTEE ON CONSUMER AFFAIRS, PRODUCT SAFETY, AND INSURANCE

OF THE

COMMITTEE ON COMMERCE, SCIENCE, AND TRANSPORTATION
UNITED STATES SENATE

ONE HUNDRED NINTH CONGRESS

FIRST SESSION

JULY 18, 2005

Printed for the use of the Committee on Commerce, Science, and Transportation

U.S. GOVERNMENT PRINTING OFFICE

27–356 PDF WASHINGTON : 2006

For sale by the Superintendent of Documents, U.S. Government Printing Office
Internet: bookstore.gpo.gov Phone: toll free (866) 512–1800; DC area (202) 512–1800
Fax: (202) 512–2250 Mail: Stop SSOP, Washington, DC 20402–0001

SENATE COMMITTEE ON COMMERCE, SCIENCE, AND TRANSPORTATION

ONE HUNDRED NINTH CONGRESS

FIRST SESSION

TED STEVENS, Alaska, *Chairman*

JOHN McCAIN, Arizona
CONRAD BURNS, Montana
TRENT LOTT, Mississippi
KAY BAILEY HUTCHISON, Texas
OLYMPIA J. SNOWE, Maine
GORDON H. SMITH, Oregon
JOHN ENSIGN, Nevada
GEORGE ALLEN, Virginia
JOHN E. SUNUNU, New Hampshire
JIM DEMINT, South Carolina
DAVID VITTER, Louisiana

DANIEL K. INOUYE, Hawaii, *Co-Chairman*
JOHN D. ROCKEFELLER IV, West Virginia
JOHN F. KERRY, Massachusetts
BYRON L. DORGAN, North Dakota
BARBARA BOXER, California
BILL NELSON, Florida
MARIA CANTWELL, Washington
FRANK R. LAUTENBERG, New Jersey
E. BENJAMIN NELSON, Nebraska
MARK PRYOR, Arkansas

LISA J. SUTHERLAND, *Republican Staff Director*
CHRISTINE DRAGER KURTH, *Republican Deputy Staff Director*
DAVID RUSSELL, *Republican Chief Counsel*
MARGARET L. CUMMISKY, *Democratic Staff Director and Chief Counsel*
SAMUEL E. WHITEHORN, *Democratic Deputy Staff Director and General Counsel*
LILA HARPER HELMS, *Democratic Policy Director*

SUBCOMMITTEE ON CONSUMER AFFAIRS, PRODUCT SAFETY, AND INSURANCE

GEORGE ALLEN, Virginia, *Chairman*

TED STEVENS, Alaska
CONRAD BURNS, Montana
JIM DEMINT, South Carolina
DAVID VITTER, Louisiana

MARK PRYOR, Arkansas, *Ranking*
DANIEL K. INOUYE, Hawaii
BARBARA BOXER, California

CONTENTS

S. 1110, THE ENGINE COOLANT AND ANTIFREEZE BITTERING AGENT ACT OF 2005

MONDAY, JULY 18, 2005

U.S. SENATE,
SUBCOMMITTEE ON CONSUMER AFFAIRS, PRODUCT SAFETY, AND INSURANCE,
COMMITTEE ON COMMERCE, SCIENCE, AND TRANSPORTATION,
Washington, DC.

The Subcommittee met, pursuant to notice, at 10 a.m. in room SR–253, Russell Senate Office Building, Hon. George Allen, Chairman of the Subcommittee, presiding.

OPENING STATEMENT OF HON. GEORGE ALLEN, U.S. SENATOR FROM VIRGINIA

Senator ALLEN. Good morning. Good morning to everyone. I call this hearing of the Senate Subcommittee on Consumer Affairs, Product Safety, and Insurance to order.

We are here to consider S. 1110, a bill entitled Engine Coolant and Antifreeze Bittering Agent Act of 2005.

First, I want to thank our Ranking Member, Senator Mark Pryor, from Arkansas, for co-sponsoring this bill with me. Thank you for your attendance and interest, and your razorback dogs that you brought here as a part of our well-behaved audience.

I also thank our witnesses. I'd like to talk to you all more afterwards. We had the K–9 in there, and everyone was in such a hubbub, it was hard to get through to you all. But I want to thank our witnesses, who come from all over the country to share with this Committee their views on this legislation.

And I also do want to thank the many citizens who have shown interest in this legislation. And I thank you all for attending.

They call this the "dog days of summer," and I guess they really are literally here in this room. And we all want dogs and animals and children to have many happy summers, and that's part of the reason for this bill, which is intended to make antifreeze a less-dangerous product throughout the United States, with national standards.

When children and animals ingest antifreeze, there is the potential that they can be seriously harmed, or, killed. Many poisonings in dogs and cats have already been reported over the years. This bill envisions a reasonable solution to avoiding these types of tragedies. By adding a bittering agent to antifreeze, we hope that antifreeze becomes unpalatable to animals and to children, and deters them from any further ingestion.

This legislation is to reduce risk, and it's also important for commerce and jobs. Radiator fluid manufacturers should be given an opportunity to comment on this legislation, because it's obviously going to affect their operations and people who work for their companies. We need to keep America's businesses more competitive. And, also, we want to make sure that prices are reasonable for customers.

I believe this bill takes into consideration all parties for reasonable government action that appears to have a consensus of support, from people who are animal owners or animal lovers, to manufacturers, to customers who would also support this idea.

I look forward to hearing from our witnesses today, to hear their perspectives regarding the desirability of this legislation.

And, with that, Senator Pryor, if you'd like to make any opening comments before I proceed to introducing our witnesses and listening to testimony, we'd love to hear from you.

Senator Pryor?

STATEMENT OF HON. MARK PRYOR, U.S. SENATOR FROM ARKANSAS

Senator PRYOR. Thank you, Mr. Chairman.

I just want to say I'm so delighted to work with you on this legislation, and I look forward to working with you to help shepherd this through the Senate and through the Congress and onto the President's desk.

This is legislation that's really a win-win situation. I know the industry, as well as various consumer groups and animal advocacy groups, et cetera—children's groups—have come together to try to find a solution that's agreeable to all. We all know the nature of the problem, and that is to children and animals, antifreeze can taste good. In fact, I think some people say it tastes a little bit like soda-pop. And so, as we all know, what happens is, maybe in the garage, a container is not tightly sealed, or there's a spill in the driveway or out on the road, or some carelessly discarded antifreeze, but, nonetheless, an animal or a child will have some exposure to it, which can have fatal consequences.

So, I just think that the fact that adding this chemical to antifreeze, for pennies a gallon, is a common-sense solution, it's one that we already know will work. This chemical we're going to talk about today, I think, is the most bitter chemical in the world, or one of the most. And so, it's already in a number of other products, and it's already proven to be very effective.

And so, Mr. Chairman, thank you for your leadership on this in helping steward this bill through the Congress.

Senator ALLEN. Thank you, Senator Pryor. And I thank you. This needs to be a bipartisan effort, and I thank you for your leadership. And we're going to work together as a team.

And before we listen to the testimony of our witnesses, let me introduce each of you briefly so that our audience here in the room know who you are.

First, I want to introduce a Representative from the State of New Mexico, Kathy McCoy, a state legislator, who flew in last night to join us. Representative McCoy was instrumental in enacting similar legislation in the State of New Mexico. She also has her own unfortunate personal story to relate.

Representative McCoy, thank you. Thank you for coming. We look forward to hearing your expert testimony, as legislators at the Federal level, to learn from what you all have done with your leadership in New Mexico.

Next, we'll hear from Jacqueline Elder, Assistant Executive Director for Hazard Identification and Reduction at the Consumer Product Safety Commission. She was present at the CPSC when a study was commissioned to study the effectiveness of bittering agents in consumer products. Her professional expertise is appreciated.

Thank you, Ms. Elder, for being here this morning.

We'll then hear from Jeff Bye, who's Vice President of Prestone, which is a subsidiary of Honeywell. Jeff's company is the largest manufacturer of antifreeze in the world.

Your testimony, Mr. Bye, will be important, because this legislation will partially and significantly fall upon your shoulders and that of your company. Thank you for being with us.

Finally, we'll hear from Sara Amundson, Deputy Director of the Doris Day Animal League. Sara's organization is a strong, respected advocate for protecting animals from preventable harm, which is, we all agree, a very worthy goal, a goal that is furthered, we believe, by this legislation.

We look forward to hearing your understanding of the way that bittering legislation has developed in the goal of making antifreeze a safer product throughout the United States.

Thank you all for being here. We'd first like to hear from Representative McCoy.

Ms. McCoy?

STATEMENT OF HON. KATHY A. McCOY, STATE REPRESENTATIVE FROM NEW MEXICO

Ms. McCoy. Thank you, Mr. Chairman, Senator.

I appreciate the opportunity to appear before you today to testify on a topic that will resonate with anyone who holds their family pets dear to them. And I also appreciate you considering this important legislation in such a thoughtful manner.

For many of us, losing a beloved family pet is like losing a member of the family. I'm here today because I lost Cujo, my golden retriever, who is pictured here, to a painful and prolonged death due to antifreeze poisoning. You have a chance today to spare other families by approving this legislation before you.

As a member of the New Mexico House of Representatives, I sponsored legislation that requires that a bittering agent, denatonium benzoate, be added to antifreeze. My own experience is what motivated me being here today. It's been over 20 years since I lost Cujo, but I've not forgotten the devastating experience. The costs are extremely high, not only financially, but emotionally. And anyone who believes that the cost to families is low on a tragedy like this would be wrong. Even that long ago, my veterinarian bill was in the hundreds of dollars, and it was money I could ill afford at the time. My dog was aggressively treated for over a week, while

I lost several days of work keeping vigil by his side. And the attempt to save him did fail.

Today, the cost of treating antifreeze poisoning begins at $500, and can go well over a thousand dollars. And, even with treatment, more often than not the pet will not survive the lethal toxins in antifreeze, which is deadly to kidney tissue. Some of the external symptoms that I saw were seizures, hypothermia, head tremors, vomiting, and coma. Ultimately, kidney failure results in death. Animals that do survive after—often have permanent kidney and brain damage. Unfortunately, families who do not have the resources to pay for treatment are forced to euthanize their pet.

Compare the cost to the pennies that it is estimated to cost manufacturers to add the denatonium benzoate to——

Senator ALLEN. Let's do this. From henceforth—let's call denatonium benzoate—

Ms. MCCOY. DB.

Senator ALLEN. DB. Can we?

Ms. MCCOY. Thank you, Senator.

Senator ALLEN. Are you agreed? All right.

Ms. MCCOY. That's fine with me. I always get tongue-twisted on that.

We'd obviously prefer not to burden the manufacturers at all, but the high cost of adding this bittering agent can only be measured by a family's pain.

Sadly, most of the poisonings are accidental. One of the most common ways for a dog to come in contact is if a family car leaks. Its sweet flavor is irresistible to most animals, and it is lethal in as little as a quarter of an ounce. For example, if a cat just walks through a puddle of it and then licks its paws, unless it has immediate veterinary care, that cat will likely die.

And since it tastes good to animals, it is also a method commonly used by some to deliberately and cruelly poison animals. Because pet owners typically don't report pet deaths due to antifreeze poisoning, I can't accurately cite any numbers of animal deaths, but I worked with our local shelter for 8 years, and I know—there's enough anecdotal evidence to know that this is a common occurrence.

I introduced this legislation in New Mexico, not only because of my personal experience, but also because of another dog, named Scooby. Scooby was also a golden retriever, and he made news in New Mexico when he was shot in the face. He managed to survive that ordeal, only to be poisoned while he was recovering. Had he not been drawn to the antifreeze, he'd still be alive, and the little girl who owned Scooby would be a happier child.

Too often, we discount animal suffering, and rationalize that "they're just animals." But they do feel pain, and they do deserve to be treated humanely. And their families deserve to enjoy their company for as long as possible.

This legislation before you is a step in eliminating one form of suffering. It's been said that the way we treat our animals is a measure of our society. Today, we have an opportunity to raise the bar of compassion a little bit higher.

In my opinion, this is win-win legislation. After getting this passed in the New Mexico House, I received an incredible amount of positive feedback. I got phone calls, letters from schools, letters from other people, and people still stop me on the street and thank me. It has no downside. It makes economical sense, and it's also the right thing to do.

So, I hope you will move this legislation forward, for those of us who have been exposed to the lethal effects of antifreeze poisoning and for those who may be exposed in the future.

Mr. Chairman and Senator, that concludes my testimony, and I would be happy to answer any questions.

Senator ALLEN. Thank you, Representative McCoy, for your testimony and your experience. We'll hear from all the witnesses, and then we'll pose questions afterwards.

[The prepared statement of Representative McCoy follows:]

PREPARED STATEMENT OF HON. KATHY A. MCCOY, STATE REPRESENTATIVE FROM NEW MEXICO

Mr. Chairman and Members of the Committee:

Thank you for the opportunity to appear before you and testify on a topic that will resonate with anyone who holds dear their family pets. And thank you for also considering this important legislation in a thoughtful manner.

For many of us, losing a beloved pet is like losing a member of the family. I'm here today because I lost my Golden Retriever, Cujo, to a painful and prolonged death due to antifreeze poisoning.

You have a chance to spare other families that tragedy by approving the legislation before you.

As a Member of the New Mexico House of Representatives, I sponsored legislation that requires that a bittering agent—denatonium benzoate—be added to antifreeze. (While the bill I sponsored passed both chambers, it was actually an identical Senate bill that was signed into law by the governor.) The experience I had with my own dog was the motivating force.

It's been over 20 years since I lost Cujo, but I've not forgotten the devastating experience. The costs are extremely high, both emotional and financial. Anyone who believes there is little cost to families who experience this tragedy is flat wrong. Even that long ago, my vet bill was hundreds of dollars, money I could ill afford at the time. My dog was aggressively treated for over a week while I lost several days of work keeping a vigil at his side. The attempt to save him failed.

Today, the cost of treating a poisoning such as this starts at $500. Even with treatment, more often than not, the pet will not survive the effects of the lethal toxins in antifreeze. Some external symptoms are seizures, hypothermia, head tremors, and vomiting. Ultimately, kidney failure results in death. Animals that do survive may suffer permanent kidney and brain damage.

And unfortunately, families who don't have the financial resources have no real choice other than euthanasia for their pet.

Compare the cost to the pennies it is estimated to cost manufacturers to add denatonium benzoate to a $7 gallon of antifreeze. We'd prefer not to burden the manufacturers at all, but the high cost of not adding this bittering agent can only be measured by a family's pain.

Sadly, most of these poisonings are accidental—one of the most common ways for animals to come in contact with antifreeze is from a family car that's leaking it. Antifreeze's sweet flavor is irresistible to most animals, and it is lethal in as little as a quarter of an ounce. For example, a cat that walks through a puddle and then licks its paws will likely die without immediate veterinary care.

And, since antifreeze tastes good to animals, it is also a method used by some to deliberately and cruelly poison animals.

Because pet owners don't typically report pet deaths due to antifreeze poisoning, I can't accurately cite the quantity of animals deaths, but having volunteered at our local shelter for eight years, I've heard enough anecdotal evidence to know that it is a common occurrence.

I introduced this legislation in New Mexico not only because of my personal experience, but also because of another dog named Scooby. Scooby, who was also a Golden Retriever, made news in New Mexico when he was shot in the face. He managed to survive that ordeal, only to be poisoned while he was recovering. Had he not been drawn to the antifreeze, he'd still be alive and the little girl who owned Scooby would be a happier child.

Too often, we discount animal suffering and rationalize that "they're just animals." But they do feel pain. They do deserve to be treated humanely. And their families deserve to enjoy their company for as long as possible. This legislation before you is a step toward eliminating one form of suffering.

It's been said that the way we treat our animals is a measure of our society; today we have an opportunity to raise the bar of compassion a little higher.

In my opinion, this is win-win legislation. After getting this passed in the House, I received an incredible amount of positive feedback—phone calls, letters, and people even now stop me on the street to thank me. This legislation has no downside—it not only makes economical sense, but it is also the right thing to do. I hope you will move this legislation forward for those of us who have already experienced the lethal effects of antifreeze poisoning and for those who may be exposed in the future.

Senator ALLEN. Now we would like to hear from Ms. Elder.

STATEMENT OF JACQUELINE ELDER, ASSISTANT EXECUTIVE DIRECTOR, HAZARD IDENTIFICATION AND REDUCTION, CONSUMER PRODUCT SAFETY COMMISSION

Ms. ELDER. Thank you, Mr. Chairman, and good morning. I'm pleased to have this opportunity to come before your Subcommittee today.

I am the Assistant Executive Director for Hazard Identification and Reduction at the U.S. Consumer Product Safety Commission, or CPSC. The CPSC is a bipartisan independent agency charged with protecting the public from unreasonable risks of serious injury or death from more than 15,000 types of consumer products under the agency's jurisdiction. The CPSC has delivered critical safety benefits to America's families and has made a significant contribution to the 30 percent decline in the rate of deaths and injuries related to hazardous consumer products. We are proud of our mission and our achievements, and we appreciate the support that Congress has extended to the agency and to its goals over the years.

In my role at the CPSC, I oversee the technical work of the agency within the directorates for epidemiology, engineering sciences, economic analysis, health sciences, and laboratory sciences. My office is responsible for the collection and analysis of death and injury data related to consumer products that can lead to the development of voluntary and mandatory product-safety standards.

Today's hearing is on S. 1110, the Engine Coolant and Antifreeze Bittering Act of 2005. This legislation amends the Federal Hazardous Substances Act, which is administered by the CPSC. The legislation would require engine coolant and antifreeze to contain a bittering agent to render those products unpalatable.

On that subject, the CPSC was directed by Congress, in the Consumer Product Safety Improvement Act of 1990, to conduct a study of aversive agents. CPSC completed that study and issued a final report on aversive agents in 1992. I will direct my comments today specifically to the findings of that 1992 report.

The CPSC defined the term "aversive," for the purpose of that study, as a substance added to a product with the intent of deterring or limiting its ingestion. In 1991, the agency conducted a literature review and requested information on aversive agents, including bittering and pungent agents, from the public in a Federal Register notice. At that time, the response to the request for information and the results of the review showed that there was a general lack of information available on aversive agents, other than one bittering agent, DB. The study found that the possible acute toxicity of DB does not appear to be a significant issue at the low levels used for aversion, such as the 30-to-50 parts-per-million range identified in the legislation. DB has been present in many household products for years. It has been required to be added to ethylene glycol-containing antifreeze by several states without documented problems.

Data concerning the effectiveness of DB to decrease the amount of a substance ingested was, and continues to be, limited. A child will likely drink some of the product in question before he or she can detect the bitter taste. For this reason, aversive agents are not recommended for use with highly toxic substances that can seriously injure or kill after one or two swallows. However, the study noted that nondrug products that required child-resistant packaging and have moderate toxicity may benefit from the addition of an aversive. Products that will not kill or severely injure in the one-to-three mouthful range, but are associated with toxicity at higher levels, were cited as the most appropriate products for aversion addition.

In this regard, the American Association of Poison Control Centers, the AAPCC, evaluated 3.8 million pediatric poisoning incidents, and subsequently recommended that aversives be added to a few selected products, including ethylene glycol, which is referred to in the legislation. The 1992 study concluded that aversives, including DB, may be an additional protective measure if found to be effective.

CPSC continues to underscore the importance of child-resistant packaging and consumer awareness of the proper handling and storage of hazardous and toxic substances in the home. The 1992 report concludes that aversives alone are not a substitute for these measures. However, aversives can be part of a comprehensive safety protocol that includes these other important components.

Each year, accidental ingestion of toxic household substances is associated with almost 30 deaths to children under age five. There are about one million calls to Poison Control Centers annually involving children under 5 years of age. The CPSC will continue to work aggressively to reduce these deaths and injuries.

We are pleased that the Committee is calling attention to these dangerous hazards, and I am pleased to answer any questions that the Senators may have regarding this important subject.

Thanks.

[The prepared statement of Ms. Elder follows:]

PREPARED STATEMENT OF JACQUELINE ELDER, ASSISTANT EXECUTIVE DIRECTOR, HAZARD IDENTIFICATION AND REDUCTION, CONSUMER PRODUCT SAFETY COMMISSION

Thank you, Mr. Chairman, and good morning. I am pleased to have this opportunity to come before your Subcommittee today. I am the Assistant Executive Director for Hazard Identification and Reduction at the U.S. Consumer Product Safety Commission or CPSC. The CPSC is a bipartisan, independent agency charged with protecting the public from unreasonable risks of serious injury or death from more than 15,000 types of consumer products under the agency's jurisdiction.

The CPSC has delivered critical safety benefits to America's families and has made a significant contribution to the 30 percent decline in the rate of deaths and injuries related to hazardous consumer products. We are proud of our mission and our achievements, and we appreciate the support that Congress has extended to the agency and to its goals over the years.

In my role at the CPSC, I oversee the technical work of the agency within the directorates for Epidemiology, Engineering Sciences, Economic Analysis, Health Sciences and Laboratory Sciences. My office is responsible for the collection and analysis of death and injury data related to consumer products that can lead to the development of voluntary and mandatory product safety standards.

Today's hearing is on S. 1110, the Engine Coolant and Antifreeze Bittering Act of 2005. This legislation amends the Federal Hazardous Substances Act which is administered by the CPSC. The legislation would require engine coolant and antifreeze to contain a bittering agent to render those products unpalatable.

On that subject, the CPSC was directed by Congress in the Consumer Product Safety Improvement Act of 1990 to conduct a study of aversive agents. CPSC completed that study and issued a final report on aversive agents in 1992, and I will direct my comments today specifically to the findings of that 1992 report.

The CPSC defined the term aversive for the purpose of that study as a substance added to a product with the intent of deterring or limiting its ingestion. In 1991, the agency conducted a literature review and requested information on aversive agents, including bittering and pungent agents, from the public in a Federal Register notice. At that time, the response to the request for information and the results of the review showed that there was a general lack of information available on aversive agents other than one bittering agent, denatonium benzoate or DB.

The study found that possible acute toxicity of DB does not appear to be a significant issue at the low levels used for aversion, such as the 30 to 50 parts per million range identified in the legislation. DB has been present in many household products for years. It has been required to be added to ethylene glycol-containing antifreeze by several states without documented problems.

Data concerning the effectiveness of DB to decrease the amount of a substance ingested was and continues to be limited. A child will likely drink some of the product in question before he or she can detect the bitter taste. For this reason aversive agents are not recommended for use with highly toxic substances that can seriously injure or kill after one or two swallows.

However, the study noted that non-drug products that require child-resistant packaging and have moderate toxicity may benefit from the addition of an aversive. Products that will not kill or severely injure in the one to three mouthful range, but are associated with toxicity at higher levels, were cited as the most appropriate products for aversion addition.

In this regard the American Association of Poison Control Centers, the AAPCC, evaluated 3.8 million pediatric poisoning incidents and subsequently recommended that aversives be added to a few selected products, including ethylene glycol, which is referenced in the legislation.

The 1992 study concluded that aversives, including DB, may be an additional protective measure if found to be effective. CPSC continues to underscore the importance of child-resistant packaging and consumer awareness of the proper handling and storage of hazardous and toxic substances in the home. The 1992 report concludes that aversives alone are not a substitute for these measures. However, aversives can be a part of a comprehensive safety protocol that includes these other important components.

Each year, accidental ingestion of toxic household substances is associated with almost thirty deaths to children under age five. There are about one million calls to Poison Control Centers annually involving children under five years of age.

The CPSC will continue to work aggressively to reduce these deaths and injuries. We are pleased that the Committee is calling attention to these dangerous hazards, and I am pleased to answer any questions that the Senators may have regarding this important subject. Thank you.

Senator ALLEN. Thank you, Ms. Elder, for your comments and your testimony.

I'm going to offer into the record this 1992 study that you referenced in your testimony. *

Senator ALLEN. I would also say, to Representative McCoy, I'm going to also enter into the record a statement of support from a mayor in your fair state, your Land of Enchantment, Mayor Cha-

---

* The information referred to has been retained in Committee files.

vez, who's the Mayor of Albuquerque. And that'll be made a part of the record, as well.

[The prepared statement of Mr. Chavés follows:]

PREPARED STATEMENT OF HON. MARTIN J. CHAVÉZ, MAYOR, ALBUQUERQUE, NEW MEXICO

Mr. Chairman, Honorable Members of the Subcommittee, thank you for this opportunity to testify on behalf of S. 1110 and the question of a bittering agent for automobile coolant.

The key ingredient in most cars' antifreeze or coolant, ethylene glycol, is deceptively sweet. So there will invariably be occasions when puddles or containers of this deadly poison are left out and accessible. Very small quantities are toxic, and sometimes lethal.

So it should come as no surprise that the American Association of Poison Control Centers reports thousands of human ethylene glycol poisonings per year, some of them fatal. According to their Annual Report for 2001, there were 4,938 human exposures to ethylene glycol, with 713 of them occurring in children under the age of 6.

The Washington State University Veterinary Medical School estimates that 10,000 dogs alone are poisoned each year. In New Mexico, the deaths of 3 children in recent years are also attributed to this poison.

Following the fatal poisoning of a local dog a couple years ago, we introduced "Scooby's Law" in Albuquerque to require that all ethylene glycol based coolant sold within the municipality include the bittering agent denatonium benzoate—also known as an "aversive" agent—to make the poison unpalatable.

Many tragedies, both locally and nationwide, could be prevented by a few drops of this bittering agent.

Denatonium benzoate has no ill effects on engine performance or cooling system life, but it can help prevent the next tragedy for a child, a pet or for nearby wildlife. It is the bitterest substance known.

After gaining feedback from the relevant business community, we passed the legislation with a phase-in timeline for vendors to comply with the new requirement. This allowed gas stations and auto parts stores to transition their shelves from existing inventory and to begin stocking the modified coolant without serious disruption or financial hardship.

The actual cost for addition of the bittering agent is estimated at about two or three cents per gallon. In the eyes of our community, it is a cost well worth bearing for the safety of our children, wildlife and pets. The feedback has been surprisingly good, and I believe even the directly involved business community has seen the virtue of the initiative.

"Scooby," the Golden Retriever who gained statewide fame by surviving a gunshot wound in the face, only to later die an excruciating death by antifreeze poisoning, highlighted the need for this common sense ounce of prevention.

California and Oregon have already passed statewide laws requiring the addition of bittering agents. And likewise we have done so in Albuquerque, as have some of our neighboring jurisdictions. But it would make much more sense to have a national standard, and that is why I am respectfully requesting that you consider making what we in Albuquerque call "Scooby's Law" the law of the land.

Thank you again for this opportunity to bring this important issue before you and thank you for your consideration.

Senator ALLEN. Mr. Bye, we'd now like to hear from you.

STATEMENT OF JEFFREY BYE, VICE PRESIDENT, PRESTONE

Mr. BYE. Thank you, Mr. Chairman, Senator Pryor.

I appreciate the opportunity to talk to you about why, from the industry side, we support Federal legislation that is both effective and efficient in getting us all where we want to be on this issue. I'd like to give you a little bit of background as to where we come from, as an industry.

I work for Prestone Products, which is part of Honeywell International. As you well know, that's a large multinational corporation, over 100,000 employees worldwide, over 50,000 employees here in the United States. We are in the transportation products group. We also manufacture and sell Fram filters, and Autolite spark plugs.

Prestone, as a brand—as a product, is the largest-selling brand of antifreeze in the United States. We produce both branded product and store-branded product for our major retail partners. We produce that product in three states—New Jersey, Illinois, and California—as well as in Mexico City, Mexico. And we distribute it through major retailers, mass merchants like Wal-Mart, Target, Kmart, automotive retailers like Advance Auto Parts, Autozone, Pep Boys, in all 50 states, as well as Canada and Mexico.

Antifreeze itself has been around since the late 1920s. Prestone started producing the product in 1927. Back then, it was purely ethylene glycol. It replaced water as a coolant/freeze protector because it has tremendous properties in heat dissipation and freeze protection. Over the years since then, Prestone has taken a leadership role, from an R&D standpoint, in putting additives into that ethylene glycol, but still maintaining ethylene glycol as the primary component of antifreeze. Those additives that we put in provide corrosion protection for cooling systems and improve the heat-and-freeze protection characteristics of the product.

To that end, although ethylene glycol is a tremendous chemical for use in a car's cooling system, it does have the downside that we're all well aware of, in that it is toxic to both people and pets. Prestone has always taken the position of doing whatever we can to provide added measures of safety. I mean, we put childproof caps on products. We put a secondary level of sealant on the product, with a foil wrap. On the animal front, we fund veterinary poison hotlines. We fund research libraries in the veterinarian community for data to get out to the community.

But, in spite of all of that, over the past X period of time there has been a movement afoot to add this bittering agent to the product, because, as Senator Pryor points out, although I can't speak from experience, it is a very sweet-tasting product, ethylene glycol, in its natural state. Back in 1992, a state bill, the first state bill, was passed in Oregon to require manufacturers to add bittering agent to deter animals from accidentally coming across or consuming the product. That was followed with another state bill, in California in 2002, requiring manufacturers to add the component. Most recently, New Mexico, as we have heard, passed legislation last year.

Our position, up until recently, had been to oppose those bills on a state level. And the reason was really twofold. Picture, if you will, that we distribute through all of those retailers I described, to 50 states. We ship product to Wal-Mart, who has 37 distribution centers, that then distributes out to over 3,000 stores. We have no way of tightly controlling that on a state-by-state basis. And our concern was, as individual states, and even municipalities, started passing legislation that were not all similar, that we could end up with, down the road, state-by-state requirements on our product that were different from other states. And that becomes very, very unworkable, and a logistical nightmare, not only for us, but for our retail partners. And, ultimately, it becomes very expensive to the end consumer, as they would end up paying a lot of those retailers' bills to redistribute that product on a state-by-state basis.

The other issue we had is the bittering agent itself. We are experts in automotive cooling systems, we are experts in the chemicals we put in to address the needs of those cooling systems that the car manufacturers produce. We are not experts in bitterants, we are not experts in the toxicity of bitterants, we are not experts in the efficacy of bitterants, and we are not experts in the long-term effects of those bitterants. So, we also opposed it on those levels. We just are not experts in that area. We don't know the impact of it.

In spite of all of that, these bills continue to gain support. There are now eight more states that are looking at legislation, all slightly different from one another. And, last year, the Conference of Mayors supported legislation, or supported a movement to pass legislation, on a municipal level.

It's our position now—and late last year, we partnered with the Doris Day group—to support this legislation, because we cannot handle state-by-state differences. Whereas, if we could get an over-arching Federal bill that would allow a uniform direction to us, as manufacturers, for what we need to do, and let us assume liability and get assigned liability for our products that we are experts at, and let the manufacturers and the providers of DB have assigned liability for whatever their products may do, or not do, it's a win for all of us. The people that are concerned about animals and their protection win; and we win, as manufacturers, because we have uniform direction on what to do; the retailers win, because they get a unified product; and the end-consumer wins, because their animals will get better protection, and they will not have to pay any additional cost for a resulting myriad of products that could result without this legislation.

So, that's our position. Again, like everyone else, we look forward to answering questions at the end.

[The prepared statement of Mr. Bye follows:]

PREPARED STATEMENT OF JEFFREY BYE, VICE PRESIDENT, PRESTONE

Good Morning. I am Jeff Bye, Vice President for Prestone, a Honeywell business. Prestone has been a leader in the manufacture, marketing and sale of antifreeze products for over 75 years. I am here representing Honeywell as well as the domestic antifreeze industry, which has been organized by the Consumer Specialty Products Association. We appear before the Committee in support of Senate bill 1110.

Honeywell is a diversified technology and manufacturing leader, serving customers with aerospace products and services; control, sensing and security technologies; automotive products; specialty chemicals; fibers; and electronic materials. Based in Morris Township, New Jersey, Honeywell's shares are traded on the New York Stock Exchange as well as on the London, Chicago and Pacific Stock Exchanges. We are one of the 30 stocks that make up the Dow Jones Industrial Average and we are also a component of the Standard & Poor's 500 Index. The company employs over 100,000 employees, with approximately 55,000 in the United States, and is comprised of four business units: Aerospace, Automation and Control Systems; Specialty Materials, and Transportation Systems. Prestone is part of the Consumer Products Group within the Transportation Systems business unit.

Honeywell is the largest manufacturer and supplier of automotive antifreeze in the United States, Canada and Mexico. Its Prestone brand is the most widely recognized and distributed brand of antifreeze in North America. In the United States, our Prestone antifreeze is sold in all 50 states and through virtually all major mass retailers, such as Wal-Mart, and auto retailers, such as Autozone and Advance. In addition, we supply private label antifreeze to most major retailers in the United

States. We also supply automakers, such as General Motors, Ford and Toyota, for the factory fill of their automobiles in North America.

It may be helpful to understand the origin of antifreeze use in the automotive industry. Originally, motorists drove cars, such as the Ford Model T, without heaters or side and rear windows and, not surprisingly, winter driving was very unpleasant. Later, with the development of car heaters, installation of side and rear windows, and improvements in engines and engine lubricants, motorists drove more comfortably and frequently in winter and demand for engine antifreeze arose. At that time, many compounds were used with water as a form of antifreeze, including honey, sugar, molasses and, the most popular, methyl alcohol. Even methyl alcohol, however, had significant drawbacks including odor and flammability. Motorists were often uncertain about freezing protection afforded by these fluids.

The antifreeze/coolant business as we know it today began with Prestone brand ethylene glycol antifreeze in 1927. It was pure ethylene glycol in cans and was packaged with charts showing the protection afforded by specific dilutions. The fluid would not evaporate or burn, was relatively odorless and offered many advantages over the substances used earlier by motorists. A few years later, Prestone developed and marketed the first inhibitor in its antifreeze to offer additional protection for the cooling system and to retard rust. In the early 1960s, Ford, General Motors and Chrysler began filling their new cars with a 50 percent ethylene glycol and 50 percent water antifreeze/coolant solution, which led to the emergence of antifreeze/coolant as a year-round functional fluid in the automotive industry. Since then, Prestone and other producers of antifreeze/coolant have developed their formulations to provide even better corrosion protection and extend the life of a car's cooling system.

Ethylene glycol, which is a major ingredient of antifreeze, is toxic. For several decades, manufacturers of antifreeze have used foil safety seals and childproof caps to guard against the accidental ingestion of antifreeze. Prestone provides prominent label warnings about proper use, storage and disposal of antifreeze. We fully comply with all child protection requirements established by the Consumer Products Safety Commission and we are dedicated to continual improvement. In addition, manufacturers have participated in public education and outreach promoting the safe use and storage of antifreeze. During the past 10 years, antifreeze manufacturers have supported the American Association of Poison Control Centers in a series of public service announcements entitled "Take Care: Car Fluids, Children and Pets." These public service announcements also help to educate consumers about proper use and storage of antifreeze and other automobile fluids.

Although it is rare that children are accidentally exposed to antifreeze, there are occasions where household pets and other animals are exposed to ethylene glycol products and are injured by ingesting the product. Some animal deaths are likely caused by intentional poisoning, such as a disgruntled person targeting a neighborhood dog that has been barking at night or causing other problems. Other animal fatalities are accidentally caused by antifreeze that has spilled or been carelessly left in improperly secured containers. We and other antifreeze manufacturers sponsor the Animal Poison Control Center of the American Society for the Prevention of Cruelty to Animals as a resource and service for veterinarians and pet owners. The Animal Poison Control Center is the leading animal-oriented poison control center in North America, with a staff of specially trained veterinary toxicologists available to handle any animal poison-related emergency, 24 hours a day, 365 days a year.

For several years, the animal rights community has encouraged local, State and Federal lawmakers to pass legislation requiring antifreeze manufacturers to add denatonium benzoate ("DB"), a widely known bittering agent, to their product. The animal rights community has argued that adding DB to antifreeze would make the product taste bitter, discouraging animals from ingesting the liquid. Their legislative efforts have met with some success, with laws passed in Oregon, California and New Mexico in 1991, 2002 and 2005, respectively.

Late last year, the antifreeze industry reached out to the Doris Day Animal League to develop consensus Federal legislation that would address the safety concerns of the animal rights community. The consensus Federal legislation—S.1110—would require the addition of DB in antifreeze with the goal of rendering the product unpalatable and deterring children, pets and other animals from accidental poisoning. This Federal legislation would create a national standard. Although California, Oregon and New Mexico have passed similar or identical laws, the legislation's preemption would avoid the potential inconsistency and practical difficulty of manufacturers complying with what could become a patchwork of various state and local mandates. At least eight other states have been actively considering similar requirements, including Massachusetts, Nebraska, Nevada, Maine, New York, New Jersey, Tennessee and Washington. Now is the appropriate time for Congress to establish a national standard before other states or localities pass inconsistent mandates.

S.1110 shares many of the essential components of the state laws as well as legislation introduced in the House of Representatives in 2004. The three state laws and H.R. 1560, sponsored in the 108th Congress by Rep. Gary Ackerman (D–NY) and Dana Rohrabacher (R–CA), all provide liability protection to antifreeze manufacturers for DB. The New Mexico law requires antifreeze manufacturers to specifically add DB as the bittering agent to their products. The laws in Oregon and California and H.R. 1560, which was cosponsored by 110 House Democrats and 23 House Republicans last year, allow alternatives to DB as the bittering additive, but DB is the only chemical that satisfies the legislations' bitterness standard at the specified concentration—thereby establishing an effective mandate requiring manufacturers to use DB to fulfill the state law requirements. H.R. 1560 was re-introduced by Reps. Ackerman and Rohrabacher this year as H.R. 2567 as the companion bill to S. 1110 and is attracting bipartisan cosponsors.

The difficulty of managing compliance with a patchwork of inconsistent state mandates could be significant and may hinder distribution of an adequate supply of antifreeze to some states. The effects of state-specific mandates could therefore be felt by individual consumers who may pay a higher cost for antifreeze and may not be able to buy enough for their needs. A national standard would ensure that the mandates are both uniform and cost effective.

The Federal legislation would also provide fair responsibility for the antifreeze and DB products by assigning liability between the respective manufacturers. Prestone scientists have developed antifreeze products that we stand behind and are willing to defend. Antifreeze manufacturers, however, do not manufacture or distribute DB. While antifreeze manufacturers are willing to add DB in compliance with a national standard, antifreeze manufacturers should not be exposed to liability for complying with that mandate. The proposed Federal legislation would not change the liability of antifreeze manufacturers for their products. Under the legislation, antifreeze manufacturers continue to be liable for the ethylene glycol antifreeze itself and DB manufacturers and distributors are liable for their bittering agent.

Honeywell, Prestone and the U.S. antifreeze industry appreciate the deliberative approach that Chairman George Allen and Ranking Member Mark Pryor have taken in regard to development of S. 1110, The Engine Coolant and Antifreeze Bittering Agent Act of 2005. We are ready to assist the Committee as it considers the legislation, and we will be happy to answer any of the Committee's questions.

Senator ALLEN. Thank you, Mr. Bye, for your testimony.

Now we'd like to hear from Ms. Amundson.

STATEMENT OF SARA AMUNDSON, LEGISLATIVE DIRECTOR, DORIS DAY ANIMAL LEAGUE

Ms. AMUNDSON. Thank you very much, Mr. Chairman and Ranking Member Pryor, for not only holding this hearing on S. 1110, but also demonstrating leadership on this particular issue that will ultimately save the lives of animals and help to prevent ingestion by children.

I'm Sara Amundson, Legislative Director for the Doris Day Animal League. We have 350,000 members nationwide who strongly support rapid movement of this bill into law. Obviously, you've heard from the panel members today that this bill enjoys broad support from a variety of animal-advocacy, public-health organizations, and also the antifreeze industry. We've traditionally been at loggerheads, as Jeff Bye just mentioned, on the state level on this issue, but enjoy the privilege of working with them to pass this bill into law.

Obviously, Honeywell is a supporter, the Consumer Specialty Products Association, the American Academy of Pediatrics, and the Pet Food Institute, in addition to our organization. Clearly, you've heard other testimony today as to the nature of the toxic antifreeze that our pets are ingesting. In addition to that, you've had a clear sense for why DB, as the most aversive bittering agent known to humankind, is really the choice of chemical to place in this particular product, so I won't repeat that particular information.

We have been tracking ingestions of antifreeze by pets and wildlife, and what we've found is that, in one survey, two out of three veterinarians see at least one ethylene glycol poisoning every single year. The Veterinary School at the Washington State University estimates the annual number of dog and cat antifreeze poisonings at as many as 10,000. And do keep in mind, with those 10,000 poisonings, the preponderance of those animals actually do die.

Fortunately, it's a little bit different situation with children. According to the statistics compiled by the American Association of Poison Control Centers, approximately 1,400 children actually ingest antifreeze each year.

These statistics are alarming, and they're certainly enough for us to want to move forward in taking action on the issue. DB is clearly the answer for antifreeze, to ensure that, at pennies per gallon, we are doing everything we can to use the tools available to us to ensure that children and pets are not ingesting antifreeze.

Jeff mentioned a little bit of information with regard to what's transpired on the state level, and I do think it's important for us to note that there are three states that currently have this law in effect. New Mexico's bill, sponsored by Representative McCoy, is exactly the same language as we're seeing on the Federal level. They've really created a high threshold for us to cross. We strongly support the pursuit of progressive policy in the states, but, because of the nature of interstate commerce, and because these poisonings occur regardless of state lines, we must pass a Federal bill to ensure that the goal of reducing antifreeze poisonings is actually realized. We must extend to each child and every animal the extra layer of protection that these states have so wisely adopted. And this is only going to be accomplished in a timely, sensible, and cost-effective manner by passing a Federal bill into law.

A product that's marketed on a national basis should have a national standard to meet, and that's why we, at the Doris Day Animal League, feel very strongly that we've got to have the Federal mandate on this issue.

Please do keep in mind that the absence of Federal law undermines the effectiveness of the existing state laws. How do we prevent antifreeze spills in California from cars driving in from the 47 other states that don't require the addition of DB to antifreeze? And the lack of uniformity, frankly, is making it very difficult to judge just how effective some of these newer state laws are.

Jeff also mentioned that the U.S. Conference of Mayors passed a resolution. That resolution was very strongly worded. They asked that Congress help protect children and animals in cities by enacting Federal legislation. I think that's a very powerful testament for why it is that we need to move forward with this Federal bill.

Representative McCoy specifically discussed an incident where her own companion animal ingested antifreeze through an accident. Oftentimes, these are accidents. But what we've found through a variety of case studies is, antifreeze, because it is toxic, it's easily available, and it's quite inexpensive, is being used, in some cases, as the tool of choice to be able to still that barking neighbor's dog that someone is gravely concerned about having to contend with. One database recently reported on cases in Iowa, Michigan, Montana, Mississippi, Texas, Florida, Missouri, and Pennsylvania as all having situations where dogs were deliberately poisoned through antifreeze.

We've also been working with a family in Georgia who very recently had two dogs deliberately killed by antifreeze ingestion from a belligerent neighbor, and we're attempting to assist them in seeking justice for these two lovely faces. These two dogs were deliberately killed by antifreeze ingestion.

More than half of all American homes actually have at least one pet. We owe it to these families to ensure we provide every available protection from antifreeze poisonings. Your legislation creates an additional tool to assist in preventing these tragedies. We respectfully request your support for passing S. 1110 into law.

And this concludes my oral testimony, but I am certainly willing to entertain any questions.

[The prepared statement of Ms. Amundson follows:]

PREPARED STATEMENT OF SARA AMUNDSON, LEGISLATIVE DIRECTOR, DORIS DAY ANIMAL LEAGUE

Good morning. Thank you Mr. Chairman and Members of the Subcommittee for the opportunity to testify today in support of the *Engine Coolant and Antifreeze Bittering Agent Act.* I am Sara Amundson, Legislative Director for the Doris Day Animal League or (DDAL). DDAL has 350,000 members and supporters nationwide who strongly support S. 1110. The organization was founded in 1987 to promote the protection of animals through legislative advocacy in the states and on the Federal level. DDAL is grateful to Chairman Allen and Ranking Member Pryor for their leadership on S. 1110, with the ultimate goal of protecting animals and children.

This bill enjoys broad support from an unlikely coalition of animal advocacy organizations, public health organizations, and the antifreeze industry. In addition to DDAL, these supporters include the American Humane Association, the Humane Society of the United States, and the Society for Animal Protective Legislation, Honeywell and the Consumer Specialties Products Association, the American Academy of Pediatrics, and the Pet Food Institute.

Animals and Children are Exposed to Antifreeze

For the past fifteen years, the DDAL has been tracking ingestions of antifreeze by pets and wildlife. Poisoning occurs with this product because it is often inadvertently spilled in our driveways or left in open containers in our garages by automotive "do-it-yourselfers." Because it is colorful and has a sweet taste, animals and children are drawn to it and may quickly ingest a lethal amount. In addition, a neighbor wishing to rid himself of a bothersome barking dog or wandering cat may purposefully bait a pet, instigating a cruel solution to a neighborhood squabble. One teaspoon of ethylene glycol antifreeze can kill a cat. Two tablespoons can kill a small, 10-pound dog. One survey found that two out of three veterinarians see at least one accidental ethylene glycol poisoning each year. The vet school at Washington State University estimates the annual number of dog and cat antifreeze poisonings at as many as 10,000. And unfortunately, the symptoms of poisoning can be misleading, causing the pet lover to think the animal is merely sleepy until renal failure causes death.

According to statistics compiled by the American Association of Poison Control Centers, as many as 1,400 children ingest antifreeze each year. The U.S. National Library of Medicine Toxicology Data Network states that the minimum lethal dose for a 150-pound male is 4 ounces, which means it takes far less to kill a child. Fortunately, in the vast majority of cases, ingestion by children is caught early enough to ensure the antidote prevents lethal consequences.

Ethylene glycol antifreeze has been manufactured for decades by the antifreeze industry and due to the ready availability of the chemical, we fully expect its continued dominance in the marketplace.

Denatonium benzoate

The good news is that, unlike many of the issues we grapple with, this one has a ready solution. DDAL certainly considers safety caps, seals and public education necessary. However, three states and several other countries have chosen to add another tool, which is requiring the addition of denatonium benzoate to antifreeze available in the consumer market. Denatonium benzoate (DB) is one of the bitterest substances known and available to us. In 1963, the Food and Drug Administration approved the addition of DB to cosmetic and toiletry products including nail polish, hair spray and cleaners as a safety mechanism to deter children from ingesting them. The U.S. Bureau of Alcohol, Tobacco, Firearms and Explosives (27 CFR 21.76) requires that all industrial alcohol-based products contain a bittering agent and specifically requires the use of DB in certain products as a denaturant, making the product unpalatable. The addition of the bitterant has not compromised the usefulness of the products.

The required addition of denatonium benzoate to consumer-packaged antifreeze will save thousands of animal lives and prevent hundreds of children from being sent to emergency rooms each year. DDAL strongly urges your support of this small measure, literally costing pennies per gallon, to achieve significant, beneficial consequences.

California State Law

The Doris Day Animal League has a long history of lobbying in support of state legislation to require the addition of denatonium benzoate to make antifreeze unpalatable to both animals and children. In 1993, in response to concerns from veterinary emergency rooms, DDAL members who had lost a beloved pet, the death of a California condor, and the startling statistics on children gathered annually by the American Association of Poison Control Centers, we successfully lobbied the California Legislature to require the addition of denatonium benzoate to antifreeze and coolant products. In spite of significant opposition mounted by the manufacturers of antifreeze, the bills passed with overwhelming votes in both the California Assembly and Senate. Unfortunately, the governor vetoed the bill.

Then in 2000, after losing her family's beloved dog Angus to antifreeze poisoning, Californian Lauren Ward began researching the solution to her family's tragedy. She contacted her state legislators to demand to know why the simple addition of DB to antifreeze to help prevent these unnecessary deaths wasn't required by the state. Fortunately, her assemblyman agreed to introduce a bill to require the bitterant be added.

Our research in support of the California bill demonstrated that in the 10 years that had passed, despite the voluntary efforts by the antifreeze industry to educate the public, there was little progress in reducing the numbers of animals and children poisoned by ingesting antifreeze. In 2001, 13 California veterinary clinics reported 136 cases of antifreeze poisoning with 107 deaths. Working with Lauren Ward and Members of the California State Senate and Assembly, we lobbied again for passage of an antifreeze bittering bill. The California Medical Association, American Academy of Pediatrics, California Veterinary Medical Association and the California Integrated Waste Management Board all supported the legislation. Over the objections of the antifreeze industry, the bill passed and was signed into law in 2002.

Subsequently, we have worked with legislators in New Mexico, Nevada, and several other states to support bills to require the addition of denatonium benzoate to antifreeze. This year, New Mexico became the third state to pass this bill into law. And the language is identical to the Federal bill before you today.

While DDAL certainly supports the pursuit of progressive policy by states, because of the nature of commerce in this country and because these poisonings occur regardless of state lines, it is imperative to pass a Federal bill to ensure that the goal of reducing antifreeze poisonings is realized. It is important to extend to each child and every animal the extra layer of protection that these states have so wisely adopted. This can be accomplished in a timely and sensible manner only through Federal action. A product marketed on a national basis should have a national standard to meet. Moreover, the absence of a Federal law undermines the effectiveness of existing state laws: The ease of interstate transportation necessitates a uniform policy to prevent antifreeze spills in California from cars driving into the state from Nevada. It is impossible to judge the effectiveness of these new state laws based on the interstate nature of the problem. In fact, the U.S. Conference of Mayors, at its 2004 annual meeting, passed a resolution urging Congress to "help cities protect children and animals by enacting legislation" to require the addition of DB to antifreeze.

Conclusion

Antifreeze poisoning causes animals great suffering, and often death. In addition to the accidents that happen, DDAL knows of numerous cases where individuals have deliberately given antifreeze to animals because they wanted to kill them. One database recently reported on cases in Iowa (where authorities at the time were investigating 8 cases), Michigan, Montana, Mississippi, Texas, Florida, Missouri and Pennsylvania. We have been working with a family in Georgia that is trying to get justice for their two dogs killed by a belligerent neighbor. And of course, Representative McCoy, who successfully carried the bill in New Mexico, lost her own companion animal in the same way.

Where the perpetrator is known, it often is a neighbor; occasionally it is an adolescent just starting down the path of antisocial behavior. They use antifreeze because it is easy to get, easy to give, and almost guaranteed to kill.

Accidents can happen despite the best prevention and precautions, and sadly there are always those who seek an easy way to harm animals. This legislation will do much to prevent both kinds of tragedies from happening.

Please support S. 1110, the *Engine Coolant and Antifreeze Bittering Agent Act.*

Senator ALLEN. Your statements will be made part of the record.

Let me start with Representative McCoy, since your legislation is the model, as far as Senator Pryor and I are concerned, for the Nation. Do you know if there are any environmental concerns associated with DB? It's important for us to understand, from your experiences, if you've heard of any environmental problems due to this additive.

Ms. MCCOY. Mr. Chairman and Senator, DB was approved in 1963, and is currently used in all types of products. It's used in paints, nail polish, household cleaners, windshield-washing fluids, deer repellent, and many others. I'm, too, very concerned about any detrimental effects to the environment. I happen to be a charter member of Republicans for Environmental Protection, so I care about these things.

But if—with your permission, I would like to share a short exchange between Nevada Senator Carlton and Vern Rossi, who is Deputy Administrator of Federal Facilities and Waste Management Programs, Division of Environmental Protection, Department of Conservation and Natural Resources.

Senator ALLEN. Boy, that's a mouthful.

Ms. MCCOY. It's a mouthful. The title is long.

[Laughter.]

Senator ALLEN. That's Federal, not Nevada, right?

Ms. MCCOY. Yes. I believe so, yes, sir. I'm just going to read the Q&A, if that's all right with you, Senator.

"Senator CARLTON. I would like Mr. Rossi to come forward with information on the environmental effects of DB.

"Mr. ROSSI. We regulate antifreeze as hazardous waste if it is not going to be recycled. If it is to be recycled, we are not concerned, because it is not going into the environment. Adding a bittering agent to antifreeze will not change regulations of those materials. The disposing or handling of antifreeze is a great concern.

"Senator CARLTON. There is some confusion about the environmental impact of DB. One group is saying there will be no impact on the environment, and the other group is saying there's a risk. If antifreeze enters a water source, it will contaminate it immediately.

"Mr. ROSSI. That is a concern. It does not matter if an additional chemical is added to antifreeze. It still has the potential to pollute a water source. Improper disposing of antifreeze is not acceptable.

"Senator CARLTON. Has there been any research on the long-term environmental effects of DB?

"Mr. ROSSI. I've not seen any data that causes me to believe that a bittering agent will add to the environmental issue.

"Senator CARLTON. Would it still be a problem with antifreeze entering groundwater, whether or not DB was added?

"Mr. ROSSI. Yes. The proper disposal of antifreeze is always a concern."

So, that—I think that exchange, coming from what I would consider a—expert testimony, speaks to the issue of environmental concerns.

Thank you, Senator.

Senator ALLEN. Thank you, Representative McCoy. That makes a great deal of sense.

Ms. Elder, you mentioned that DB has been in household products for, really, decades now. Is there any evidence that DB has caused any harm by being added to products like paint to keep children from eating that, or nail polish or other products?

Ms. ELDER. Are you speaking specifically of environmental types of issues?

Senator ALLEN. Right. Environmental or any other added hazard or risk by having that bittering agent in a household product.

Ms. ELDER. We did note, in the study that we did, that we weren't able to identify any instances of environmental damage. We did note, also, that DB does not completely biodegrade and that the effects on groundwater were unknown. But those environmental issues are probably best handled by the Environmental Protection Agency, who would have much more expertise in that area.

Senator ALLEN. Well, you mentioned there's no documented problems in the states that have required the addition of DB to their antifreeze. Is there any reason to suspect that that would change if we had Federal national legislation?

Ms. ELDER. No. The data that we have is limited, and we just don't know that.

Senator ALLEN. All right, thank you.

Mr. Bye, you all have changed your positions on this issue, from years ago. Let me ask you this. It's good to know Honeywell, or Prestone, is in favor of this legislation. Is the entire retail antifreeze industry in support of this legislation?

Mr. BYE. Yes, they are, in fact. The domestic producers are all in favor of this, primarily for the reason I said, just from a pure logistics and operational standpoint. If we were to get to the point where different states required different products—either with a different bittering agent, with different amounts of bittering agents—it would become a very, very difficult situation in the way that we do business. So, to that end, we are all in favor of it.

Senator ALLEN. Does Honeywell or Prestone have a concern about additional cost since they do not manufacture DB. You're talking about this costing, what, pennies per gallon?

Mr. BYE. Correct.

Senator ALLEN. Could you give us the exact range, so we know? What does a gallon of antifreeze cost, presently?

Mr. BYE. There's a long——

Senator ALLEN. Not subject to——

Mr. BYE.—answer and a short answer.

Senator ALLEN.—sales taxes and all the other things that get added on, but——

Mr. BYE. It costs, plus or minus, four to six dollars, depending upon the price of ethylene glycol, which is a commodity. The DB, as we use it today, because we do put it in for the states required, is less than three cents a gallon.

Senator ALLEN. Three cents a gallon.

Mr. BYE. Correct.

Senator ALLEN. Less than.

Mr. BYE. Yes.

Senator ALLEN. All right. Are you concerned that the cost for this product will go up? Could there be a monopoly for those who manufacture DB?

Mr. BYE. I don't think so, only because—and I'll speak, again, to our source from it—we buy it from a domestic source who also supplies a number of those other inhibitors that I mentioned that go into antifreeze for corrosion protection and what have you. And the DB that we purchase is, far and away, the smallest component that we buy from this company, and would buy from the other companies. So, I think if there were included across the board, (a) you're still talking about a very small amount. It would still be considerably less than the other products we buy from them, so we would have that leverage. And you would create competition, I would think, among the other suppliers of DB, because there are other suppliers. So, I think, in general, we wouldn't see any issue with that.

Senator ALLEN. Also, let me ask you this. In three states that require this DB—and New Mexico is the model state law—has there been any harm caused to car engines, like corrosion, due to the addition of DB to the antifreeze?

Mr. BYE. No, none that we're aware of. And we've tested DB in cooling systems to understand its performance in a cooling system—again, not to its performance as a bitterant—and that is another area of concern for us, because if we were to get into other bittering agents that may be out there, they have not been tested for their performance in automotive cooling systems. So, we're very comfortable with DB, on that front.

Senator ALLEN. All right. So, there are other bittering agents. And so, DB, at least has been tested out, proven not to be any additional risk to the environment or added health risk to it, and also not harming the engine—or the radiator cooling——

Mr. BYE. Our concern is harming the engines, and we see no effects of it.

Senator ALLEN. Ms. Amundson, are you aware of any problems with respect to human health or the environment related to DB, since you all have been such strong advocates for a long while on this?

Ms. AMUNDSON. No, we certainly are not, and would be gravely concerned if there were issues related to environmental degradation.

I'm going to read, if I may, into the record from a report that was commissioned by the California Integrated Waste Management Board in 2001, when they took a very careful look at the potential for adding DB into antifreeze in the State of California. And they did, in fact, support that particular bill.

They state, through a staff study, that DB, "readily biodegrades. Its transport is attenuated by soil, and it is easily treated in sewage-treatment systems and drinking-water systems. Staff has determined that the addition of DB to antifreeze would not lead to any adverse health or environmental effects."

Senator ALLEN. What was that report, again, Ms. Amundson?

Ms. AMUNDSON. That is the 2001 California Integrated Waste Management Board, the entity for really ascertaining how to dispose of waste, and that would include chemical waste.

Senator ALLEN. Thank you. If you could provide that to the Committee, I'd like to make that report a part of the record.

Thank you.

[The information referred to follows:]

CALIFORNIA INTEGRATED WASTE MANAGEMENT BOARD,
Board Meeting, July 25–26, 2001.

AGENDA ITEM 2

Item

Consideration Of Staff Recommendations For Addressing The Impacts Of Antifreeze On Public Health And Safety In California

I. Summary

This item presents staff's recommendations to reduce the impact on health and safety that occurs from the use of antifreeze coolant in California. The most commonly used antifreeze in California is formulated with ethylene glycol, which is poisonous. Antifreeze products have a sweet taste and appealing color that may be attractive to animals and children. Drinking as little as one or two ounces can lead to death in a small child. A cat can receive a lethal dose from licking its paws after walking through spilled antifreeze. Improper storage or handling of antifreeze contributes to hundreds of human exposures in the state annually. Leaks from improperly maintained motor vehicles and improper storage and disposal leads to thousands of animal exposures each year. In addition, this product is effective and easy to use for intentional poisoning of domestic animals and wildlife.

Two methods are available to reduce or eliminate the hazards of ethylene glycol based antifreeze to humans, while providing comparable product performance. One is to add an aversive agent to ethylene glycol antifreeze to deter ingestion. The state of Oregon requires the addition of the aversive agent denatonium benzoate to ethylene glycol based antifreeze sold at the retail level. Other countries also require the addition of this bittering agent to ethylene glycol based antifreeze. California legislation was introduced in 1993 to require the addition of a bittering agent to ethylene glycol antifreeze products. The governor vetoed the bill.

Another method to reduce poisoning from antifreeze exposures is to eliminate the use of ethylene glycol based antifreeze and replace it with the much less toxic propylene glycol formulated antifreeze. The chemical propylene glycol is used in numerous prepared foods and medicines and is a common food additive. Propylene glycol based antifreeze was introduced to the California market in 1994 and is readily available, currently constituting about 5 percent of the market. Propylene glycol based antifreeze provides comparable product performance as the ethylene glycol based antifreeze. The leading antifreeze manufacturer, Prestone, offers a propylene glycol based antifreeze marketed under the brand name *LowTox*, and Old World Industries produces the *Sierra* brand. Both are sold throughout the state at competitive prices to ethylene glycol antifreeze. At least two other countries require the retail sale of propylene glycol based antifreeze as a safer substitute.

Antifreeze manufacturers oppose replacing ethylene glycol based antifreeze with propylene glycol based antifreeze or to adding an aversive agent to ethylene glycol based antifreeze. The requirement of the child resistant caps is cited as having reduced poisonings. Industry does support public education efforts to prevent exposures and poisonings. The greater chemical industry produced a video on safe use, storage and disposal of antifreeze several years ago, and may develop a new video in the next few months. Significant public education may reduce the number of exposures. The incidence of poisonings to children and adults, domestic animals and wildlife would be further diminished if reformulation or the addition of an aversive agent is required.

Staff recognize that there are significant barriers to the conversion from ethylene glycol to propylene glycol based antifreeze. While propylene glycol would provide the greatest protection, staff recommend that the addition of aversive agents be required for all ethylene glycol antifreeze products. No significant barriers to the immediate addition of the aversive agent, denatonium benzoate were identified.

II. Previous Board Action

At the January 2000 meeting, the California Integrated Waste Management Board (Board) directed staff to review methods to significantly reduce the number of human and animal poisonings from antifreeze exposures. Then at the August 2000 Board meeting, staff presented background information and findings from research and discussions with antifreeze industry representatives. Numerous options to address the antifreeze poisoning problem were presented to the Board. The Board directed staff to continue researching the highest options presented for reducing poisonings from antifreeze use and to return with recommended actions.

III. Options for the Board

Board Members may consider one or more of the following actions:

1. Direct staff to develop a legislative proposal to phase in a ban on the sale of ethylene glycol formulated antifreeze and promote the use of propylene glycol formulated antifreeze or other significantly less toxic alternatives.
2. Direct staff to develop a legislative proposal to require the addition of an aversive agent, such as denatonium benzoate, to ethylene glycol based antifreeze.
3. Direct staff to study the issues further and bring back recommendations for consideration in the future.

IV. Staff Recommendation

Staff recommends that the Board approve Option 2 as the most prudent way to protect human health and safety and reduce animal poisonings in California.

V. Analysis

Background

The Board directed staff to review methods to significantly reduce the number of human and animal poisonings from antifreeze exposures at the January 2000, meeting. Staff proceeded to interview chemical and antifreeze manufacturers, recyclers, local and state government, automotive manufacturers and service representatives and veterinary and other medical professionals. A task force meeting was held September 28, 2000. Staff researched issues raised by all parties. The goal was to investigate changes that could be made to reduce the effects caused by ethylene glycol based antifreeze exposures.

The antifreeze manufacturing industry is opposed to mandating propylene glycol based antifreeze to replace ethylene glycol antifreeze or adding an aversive agent to ethylene glycol antifreeze. In addition to child resistant caps, which has reduced poisoning incidences, industry advocates public education as the most appropriate mechanism to further decrease poisoning exposures. Industry produced a public service announcement several years ago, and has played it through television station and cable systems throughout the country including California. They are now planning to produce a new California specific video, which will replace the original video. Industry would like the Board to endorse the video. Staff has recommended that the 1–800–CLEANUP number be included in the video; however, further support and/or involvement would be at the Board's discretion.

Staff produced an in-house fact sheet on antifreeze about five years ago. Staff is revising the fact sheet to provide stronger messages to reduce accidental child and pet exposures. The fact sheet will provide additional information on the safe storage and use of antifreeze and a description of the safer propylene glycol based alternative. Staff will also work with household hazardous waste coordinators to encourage them to increase promotion of the safer antifreeze (e.g., signs placed at the point of purchase indicating that a product is an alternative to a more hazardous product).

Staff is working with the California Poison Control System (CPCS) to obtain information on the circumstances surrounding childrens' exposures. By examining exposures, staff can provide better outreach to local government household hazardous waste program coordinators and to residents. In addition, staff will provide local household hazardous waste program managers information about the services provided by CPCS.

Key Issues:

Ethylene Glycol Toxicity and Antifreeze Exposures

Ethylene glycol is an odorless, sweet tasting poisonous chemical used in the production of antifreeze and many other products. Ethylene glycol can adversely affect humans through ingestion, inhalation or contact with the eyes and/or skin. Exposures and poisonings from ethylene glycol based antifreeze are regularly reported to poison control centers. In 2000, 564 calls were made to the California Poison Control System hotline regarding ethylene glycol based antifreeze. Past statistics in California have not been comprehensively available so a trend of exposures is not available. Nationally, there were 5,376 human exposures with nine deaths in 1998 caused by ethylene glycol antifreeze. Unintentional exposures accounted for 4,932 of the cases.

According to the U.S. National Library of Medicine's Toxicology Data Network, for a 150 pound adult the minimum lethal dose of ethylene glycol is 100 ml or 4 ounces, while propylene glycol's minimum fatal dose level is probably over 32 ounces. There is an antidote for ethylene glycol antifreeze poisoning called Antizol. However, an antidote treated patient still may have to be managed for other life threatening conditions that may arise.

A much lower dose of ethylene glycol based antifreeze can kill animals with as little as one teaspoon for a cat and two tablespoons for a 10-pound dog. Animal exposures are more difficult to quantify because veterinarians are not required to report these poisoning occurrences. Reported poisonings include wild and domesticated animals, with some documented intentional poisonings. Some wild animals such as marmots have been known to chew through vehicle coolant hoses, while dogs have been known to chew the necks of antifreeze containers and ingest the antifreeze. In 1993, a California condor, an endangered species, died from ingestion of ethylene glycol.

In 1996 the American Society for the Prevention of Cruelty to Animals conducted a phone survey of animal care professionals and concluded that 118,000 domestic animals were poisoned in the U.S. by spilled or discarded antifreeze. The National Animal Poison Control Center believes that this figure is greatly exaggerated. A more conservative estimate of animal poisoning exposures is from Washington State University Veterinary Medicine School with at least 10,000 dog poisonings annually. Diagnosis and treatment of a pet ingestion of ethylene glycol based antifreeze can be delayed due to misleading symptoms. For example, a dog would get sick after ingesting antifreeze, and then appear to improve. Meanwhile, renal failure occurs and it is too late to save the dog.

Leaks from improperly maintained motor vehicles and improper storage of antifreeze as well as illegal disposal leads to thousands of animals' exposures each year. A national survey found that two out of three veterinarians see at least one accidental ethylene glycol animal poisoning each year. This would amount to over 7,000 poisoning exposures in California alone. This may be a conservative estimate because there certainly are animals that do not survive to return home and wildlife that will not have a chance to receive medical treatment. (And though the California Poison Control System hotline is not for animal emergencies, 53 calls were made regarding pets with one death documented in 2000.)

Appearing like common beverages, the attractiveness of antifreeze is a significant concern. Antifreeze comes in bright colors, similar to beverages such as Kool-Aid and Gatorade that are recognized by children. Industry indicated that the colors used in antifreeze products are market driven, so that service providers can quickly identify the types of antifreeze or other fluids they are installing. Because of worldwide distribution, changing the color or appearance of antifreeze does not appear to be a reasonable undertaking at this time.

Environmentally, both types of antifreeze biodegrade fairly rapidly—in as few as several days depending upon conditions. (Heavy metals from vehicle engines do, however, remain in the environment after the antifreeze breaks down.)

Option 1—Propylene Glycol Alternative

Propylene glycol based antifreeze is an alternative to ethylene glycol based antifreeze, and has a significantly lower degree of toxicity to humans and animals. Used in a variety of consumer products, propylene glycol is also added to food products and is listed by the U.S. Food and Drug Administration as either approved as a food additive or listed or affirmed as Generally Recognized As Safe (GRAS). Taken internally, a small amount of propylene glycol is harmless to humans. Though not considered GRAS for cats, the degree of toxicity to this species is significantly reduced compared to ethylene glycol ingestion. There is no language on either Low Tox or the Sierra brands of propylene glycol based antifreeze container labels to indicate that consumers need restrict its use for any vehicle type. There is also no language (such as special formulations required by some auto manufacturers) for restrictive use for any vehicle type on the ethylene glycol based antifreeze product containers either. Propylene glycol based antifreeze is commonly used in marine vessels as well as recreational vehicles throughout the country. Some auto manufacturers, however, do caution the consumer in the owner's manual to use the manufacturer's own brand of antifreeze because of special additives and formulations. Though one auto manufacturer indicated in the owner's manual that it is necessary to use their brand of antifreeze, and non-use could void its warranty, the same manufacturer stated that it is rare to void a warranty by use of a fluid. Another manufacturer does not promote propylene glycol based antifreeze but has accepted it, and along with other automotive manufacturers state its use would not void their warranties. And although no auto dealership surveyed installed propylene glycol based antifreeze, some of them will, upon owner request, put it in vehicles.

Propylene glycol based antifreeze is used extensively in Austria and Switzerland, where it is the only antifreeze sold at the retail level. In France and Italy, only propylene glycol based antifreeze is sold in those stores that also sell food.

Industry concerns not addressed above are outlined below in bold, followed by information gathered by staff in response:

1. **The performance capabilities of propylene glycol based antifreeze in automotive vehicles are not adequate.** The propylene glycol based antifreeze on the market currently meets the American Society for Testing and Materials (ASTM) standards for cars and light duty trucks as well as for heavy-duty vehicles.

2. **There are no "extended life" propylene glycol antifreeze formulations available.** Extended life antifreeze has only been available for several years and is a small but growing segment of the market. Propylene glycol manufacturers say the market for these formulas has not been large enough to warrant manufacturing such products, however, a propylene glycol based antifreeze extended life package can be made.

3. **Replacing all ethylene glycol based antifreeze with propylene glycol based antifreeze in California would create market problems.** The California market for antifreeze is about 20 million gallons per year. That amount constitutes about 40 percent of the total propylene glycol produced in the U.S. annually. A phased approach would be necessary to maintain supply and market stability as well as to allow time to test and approve special formulations.

4. **A rapid market swing from ethylene glycol based to propylene based antifreeze would impact the market for recycled ethylene glycol.** Auto manufacturers recommend that antifreeze be changed every few years depending on vehicle use. Because of the time between full market availability of propylene based antifreeze and the years between change-outs, the waste stream will contain significant amounts of ethylene glycol for many years. A "phased in mandate" approach would maintain a stable market for ethylene glycol as the proportion of propylene glycol to ethylene glycol increases in the antifreeze waste stream.

5. **Recycled ethylene glycol can not contain more than 15 percent propylene glycol and meet the market standard.** Currently, the antifreeze waste stream contains about 5 percent propylene glycol based antifreeze. However, recycling propylene glycol based antifreeze only allows 1 percent of other glycols to be added to it. Following a mandate to reformulate with propylene glycol, the antifreeze waste stream will contain increasing amounts of propylene glycol. Generators may need to segregate the two types of waste antifreezes with separate storage tanks needed for recyclers. Alternatively, recyclers would need to install systems to separate propylene glycol and ethylene glycol. In any case there would be significant cost involved.

6. **Topping off autos running on ethylene glycol based antifreeze with propylene glycol based antifreeze will lead to compatibility problems.** Antifreeze manufacturers and auto manufacturers are concerned that mixing two types

of formulations in a vehicle may lead to reduced performance or even failure of cooling systems because of possible incompatibility of additives.

7. **Propylene glycol costs significantly more than ethylene glycol and industry profit margins are already slim.** The retail cost of the two types of antifreeze overlap. Retail ethylene glycol based antifreeze costs $4.00–$6.00 per gallon while propylene glycol based antifreeze costs $4.50–$7.00 per gallon. Any increase in costs would be passed onto the consumers resulting in a level playing field for manufacturers.

Option 2—Aversive Agent Alternative

The other alternative to reduce poisonings from the ingestion of ethylene glycol is to add an aversive agent. Denatonium benzoate is considered the most bitter substance known. From studies reviewed, it is highly effective for humans; and dogs have exhibited symptoms of grimacing, gagging and even vomiting upon ingestion of products containing denatonium benzoate. The taste of the agent may not repel all animals, but the American Association of Poison Control Centers has recommended that aversive agents be added to ethylene glycol products. Aversive agents are currently used in other household products including pesticides to deter ingestion. Industry is concerned that if an aversive agent were added to ethylene glycol based antifreeze, consumers would be less vigilant in storing and managing the product. Staff does not necessarily agree. However, even if the number of exposures does not decrease, the amount of product ingested will decrease.

Addition of denatonium benzoate is very inexpensive, costing $0.02–$0.03 per gallon of a $5 per gallon product. Addition of denatonium benzoate to the approximately 20 million gallons of antifreeze used in California would cost about $500,000 a year. This cost is relatively small compared to the $100 million dollar market and the cost would be passed on to consumers. This amount is also small compared to the medical costs and work time lost as well as suffering that occurs from exposures to this product

Denatonium benzoate readily biodegrades, its transport is attenuated by soil, and it is easily treated in sewage treatment systems and drinking water systems. Staff has determined that the addition of denatonium benzoate to antifreeze would not lead to any adverse health or environmental effects.

The State of Oregon passed a bill in 1993 that requires the addition of a bittering agent in ethylene glycol antifreeze sold at the retail level. A similar bill was vetoed by the Governor in California in 1993. His veto message said denatonium benzoate would not decrease the number of exposures to the product and it had not been proven effective as an animal deterrent. He also said that it was premature for the state to require manufacturers add bittering agents to products before these substances are fully evaluated and determined to be effective. In response, staff note that the addition of denatonium benzoate may not prevent exposures, but it would significantly reduce the amount ingested, hence the severity of exposures. Numerous studies have shown that it does repel animals, though until it is used extensively in antifreeze, the magnitude of its effectiveness for animals in ethylene glycol based antifreeze will be difficult to verify. (Comparatively, it took 17 years to conclusively prove that child-resistant caps were effective in reducing child exposures in general.)

Denatonium benzoate is required to be added to ethylene glycol based antifreeze in the United Kingdom, Japan, and Australia. There is also currently one ethylene glycol antifreeze manufacturer in this country that voluntarily adds denatonium benzoate to their aftermarket antifreeze products (5 percent of all antifreeze currently used in the United States). Lastly, Massachusetts has introduced a bill to require the addition of denatonium benzoate to all ethylene glycol based antifreeze in their state.

Fiscal Impacts—N/A.

Findings

The lethal oral dose of ethylene glycol is a factor of over eight smaller than propylene glycol for humans, making this a compelling argument for its use. And though wide use of propylene glycol based antifreeze could prevent a majority of unintentional animal and human poisonings, mandating a change at this time to propylene glycol based formulations will cause significant industry hardship.

Addition of an aversive bittering agent, such as denatonium benzoate, would reduce human poisonings and likely prevent a significant number of animal poisonings. The addition of denatonium benzoate is relatively inexpensive and would be simple for industry to implement. There appear to be no compelling reasons not to mandate the addition of denatonium benzoate to all ethylene glycol based products. The health and safety of all residents and pets and wildlife of the state can benefit from this endeavor.

VI. Funding Information—N/A.

Senator ALLEN. Senator Pryor?

Senator PRYOR. Thank you, Mr. Chairman.

One thing I want to do today—you all know I support the legislation, but I want to ask some hard questions, because Senator Allen and I know that our colleagues will ask us these hard questions, and I'd like to get your answers on these. He's already asked some of them.

But, Mr. Bye, if I can start with you, I know that one option in framing this legislation would be that you could use either DB or some other bittering agent. And I think you mentioned, a few moments ago, that other bittering agents have not been approved, or have not been tested in automotive—in an automotive system like what you have with DB. But are there other reasons why we shouldn't expand this to DB and other agents?

Mr. BYE. All I can speak to—again, we are far from being experts in the world of bitterants. Maybe one of the other panelists would have a deeper point of view on this, but we've really just been trying to work with them in the bitterants that they feel are the most effective and most—strongest bittering agent there is, as you pointed out earlier. So, that's really all we've done, is follow their lead that that is the one to use, and, therefore, that is the one we've tested, because we produce it, in a cooling system. But, beyond that, we haven't really looked at any other bittering agents, just been doing what they've been asking us to do.

Senator PRYOR. OK, great. Let me followup on another one of Senator Allen's questions. A few moments ago he asked about DB and other sources of it. And, just to be clear, as I understand it, DB is not proprietary. In other words, it's out there in the public domain. Is that your understanding?

Mr. BYE. That's my understanding.

Senator PRYOR. And there either are now, or could be, multiple sources for DB.

Mr. BYE. I know of at least three today.

Senator PRYOR. That exist today? OK, great.

Ms. Amundson, let me ask you a question. And it's just a concern that some people might have that if you add this bittering agent, somehow maybe the industry or the word might get out that suddenly antifreeze is safe—so-called "safe"—and people might get complacent about the storage of it or the disposal of it. Do you have any comments on that?

Ms. AMUNDSON. I greatly appreciate the question. It's certainly the position of the Doris Day Animal League that we bear a responsibility to consumers to provide the information that's necessary to them to take a careful look at this issue. And, in doing so, we have never positioned ourselves as supporting the addition of DB to antifreeze as the panacea to the problem.

That said, I think we need to be careful when we're assessing these sorts of mandates, or even enforcing these sorts of mandates, on the regulated industries. Let's keep in mind the simple fact that seatbelts certainly save lives, but they don't save every life. And, unfortunately, childproof safety caps have been very successful in saving children's lives, but, if improperly used, clearly there may still be some difficulties there.

Our position has been, we need to use all the tools available to us—and that is foil seals, childproof safety caps, the addition of DB, and good, solid public education—to ensure that people still recognize that ethylene glycol antifreeze is a toxic chemical.

Senator PRYOR. OK, great.

Let me ask, too, we mentioned—Senator Allen mentioned these two different reports. There's one in 1992 from the Consumer Products Safety Commission, and there's also one in 2001 from California. I'd just like to ask the panel generally—all of you all can answer this, if you want—what is the difference in those reports? It seems to me that, if you look at them, the 2001 report is a much better, much stronger report for the position that DB is OK and this actually is a good idea. Can I—whoever——

Yes?

Ms. MCCOY. Mr. Chairman, Senator, I guess I would just simplify it by stating that antifreeze has to be properly disposed of, already. If it's—even with the bittering agent, it's—which is, I believe, 30-to-one-million parts, it's a very minute amount, so—I'm not diminishing the fact that there could be some environmental issue, but I personally did a lot of research, and had our legislature look for me, and no one could find anything definitive about it.

So, given the fact that it has to be properly disposed of without the bittering agent, I think that that's the answer. So—Thank you, Senator.

Senator PRYOR. OK. Anybody else want to comment on the two reports?

Ms. AMUNDSON. If I may, thank you.

I will say that my comprehension of the CPSC's report is that they were asked to take a very careful, narrow look at a couple of different potentials for bittering agents, and the conclusions in that report clearly stated that their recommendation was that DB be added to some consumer products, and antifreeze was one of them. While there may be information that is not necessarily collated in that report, I think the reflection of the 2001 report from the California Integrated Waste Management Board provides us with more comprehensive information on some of the questions that you're raising today, and that is because it is their job to take a careful look at what environmental consequences are going to be. And they were taking a look at this issue specifically by raising the question, What can we do with antifreeze to try to ensure that kids and animals are not ingesting it? And their conclusion clearly was to support the California bill.

Senator PRYOR. As part of these studies, have they studied whether, when you add DB, actually you see child deaths go down? Has anyone done that detail of study? Do you know? My sense is, that may be beyond the scope of any study that's been done.

Ms. AMUNDSON. Senator, I would say it's probably beyond the scope of existing studies. But I think it's a careful point that we need to make here, and that is, fortunately there are not a lot of children who do actually die from ingesting antifreeze. It is much more on the animal side.

Senator PRYOR. And I know—as I understand it, DB has been used in antifreeze for some time in the United Kingdom, Japan, and Australia. Do we know—do we have studies from those countries? And do we have data and information from those countries? Does anybody know?

[No response.]

Senator PRYOR. I'm not aware of any. I think our staff was looking for some, but I'm not aware of any.

Senator ALLEN. Mr. Bye, do you all sell—excuse me.

Senator PRYOR. Go ahead.

Senator ALLEN. Do you all sell in these countries? Japan? Australia has a lot of animals.

Mr. BYE. We sell almost no antifreeze outside of the United States. We sell mostly to retail, and outside of the United States it's not a big retail market, so we sell less than 1 percent of our sales outside the United States.

Senator PRYOR. OK. And, Mr. Bye, let me ask you, I've heard the figure "30 parts per million." What is that, about a drop per gallon?

Mr. BYE. It's a minuscule amount. I'm not a chemist, but it's a tiny amount, and—but that tiny amount is highly effective, as one who tasted bitterant the other day in a minuscule amount. And you don't ever want to do that again.

[Laughter.]

Senator PRYOR. Let me ask you——

Mr. BYE. I just wanted to be prepared.

[Laughter.]

Senator PRYOR. Yeah, great. You didn't bring any for us to drink today.

[Laughter.]

Mr. BYE. Be careful.

[Laughter.]

Senator PRYOR. Let me ask you, Mr. Bye, while we have you here, part of your company's support for this legislation is some—there's a provision that you will not be held liable under the law. Could you explain your company's rationale, what you accomplish by that?

Mr. BYE. Sure. It's, I think, pretty straightforward. We are, again, experts at the product we make, prior to bitterant, and the inhibitors and chemicals therein, in the antifreeze, and their effect and what they're designed to do in a car's cooling system. And, to that end, we're more than happy, and always have taken full—and assumed full responsibility for any liability of those products.

But we are not experts, and have had no reason to be experts in the world of bitterants, much like any other chemical. In this case, no pun intended, we become the "vehicle" for delivering that and what it does, but we've never had a reason to understand its properties, in any great detail.

And so, for that end, I think just to make this whole thing work we would be happy to assume liability for our end of the product line, and hope that the people that provide that—because it is not part of a car's cooling system—would assume liability for their end and achieve what these people are looking for.

Senator PRYOR. OK. Would your company, or would the industry, be comfortable with a sunset on that liability provision in 10 or 15 years, or not?

Mr. BYE. To be honest with you, we haven't talked about that, because we've always assumed that it would be something that would be separated from us. We could get back to you on that and look at that, but we have no position on that, currently.

Senator PRYOR. OK. And, also in terms of the industry, you maybe heard my question a few moments ago about—maybe the industry, or at least maybe the public perceiving—if the industry doesn't market it this way—but the public perceiving that somehow—by adding this chemical, that suddenly antifreeze becomes "safe." Do you—has the industry thought about that, and thought about how they market it in such a way that the public will not be misled and will understand this is still a very dangerous product, just that it is—you've added a safety feature to it? What's your—how are you going to handle that?

Mr. BYE. Sure. I would take the same position we've taken right along. And, as I mentioned in my earlier testimony, we've been supporters of the veterinary poison hotlines, and they would not want us to promote the fact that there is bitterant in the product, because it could lead to, sort of, a lax'd attitude, in their opinion. And we would fully support that. We would have no intentions of promoting the fact that their product was bittered. We would have no intentions of marketing it as a "safer" product. We would be doing it just for the case, as stated, that accidental spillages came in contact with an animal, and hope to deter them. But we wouldn't make any more point of it than that.

Senator PRYOR. And my last question—and maybe, Mr. Bye, you're the best, but whoever wants to try to answer this—is DB, itself, a toxin? Is it, in and of itself, poisonous or harmful to humans, do we know?

Mr. BYE. I don't know.

Ms. MCCOY. Mr. Chairman, Senator, I just read something recently, that a diluted form of DB is actually used as a deterrent for thumb-sucking, so, it's—I don't think it is toxic. So——

Senator PRYOR. Does anybody else have any comments on that?

Ms. ELDER. Our data shows that—at the levels that would be used for an aversive or bittering agent, that it would not have acute toxicity.

Senator PRYOR. OK. Thank you for your time.

Thank you.

Senator ALLEN. Through? Well, all right. Well, thank you, Senator Pryor, for those questions.

And I want to thank all of our witnesses for appearing today.

From this hearing—the value of hearings is to adduce testimony and information and evidence that bolster or possibly modify legislation. It strikes me that what we have here is a consensus—consensus that adding DB to antifreeze would cost less than three cents a gallon—since I'm very frugal and always look at what the cost of things are. But for less than three cents a gallon, it is not going to eliminate risk, but it is going to reduce risk. That's a key thing from Senator Pryor's questions. And some of the testimony here is, you can add a bitterant to antifreeze, but it doesn't mean that you don't have to have the same cautions, as far as caps and warnings, and, obviously, also disposal. Representative McCoy's logic was just plain old common sense, you're still going to have to dispose of itssafely. It doesn't matter whether there's a bitterant or not in it. And by reducing this risk, we clearly are going to lessen and prevent harm somewhat to humans. But the greatest risk is to animals. The references to pets—people pay attention to when their dog or cat's gone, but there are also a lot of other animals out there. There's birds, fox, deer, other—that might lap some of that up in a driveway or somewhere else, and those don't get, necessarily, reported.

The added point is, for less than three cents a gallon, reducing risk and harm to animals and humans, there's also no evidence that this will cause any environmental harm.

Its seems to me, Senator Pryor, that we need to be moving on this. We've heard some very reasoned, logical analysis here today. Thank you all, all of our witnesses, for coming from all across the country and sharing your insight and also your passion, your passion for this. And we want to thank our friends from the Land of Enchantment for showing us the way here in Washington, D.C.

Ms. McCoy. Thank you, Senator.

Senator Allen. With that, I wish you all safe travels home. Hearing adjourned.

[Whereupon, at 10:55 a.m., the hearing was adjourned.]

○

CPSIA information can be obtained at www.ICGtesting.com
Printed in the USA
BVOW10s1719121113

336108BV00007B/226/P

9 781240 519538